AROUND
PEND[LE]

SHORT ·
WAL[KS]

PAUL HANNON

HILLSIDE PUBLICATIONS
20 Wheathead Crescent
Keighley
West Yorkshire
BD22 6LX

First Published 2010

© Paul Hannon 2010

ISBN 978 1 907626 02 9

The sketch maps are based on 1947 OS one-inch maps and earlier OS six-inch maps

Cover illustration: Pendle Hill from above Barley
Back cover: Roger Moor, above Kelbrook
Page 1: At Newchurch
(Paul Hannon/Hillslides Picture Library)

Printed by Steffprint
Unit 5, Keighley Industrial Park
Royd Ings Avenue
Keighley
West Yorkshire
BD21 4DZ

CONTENTS

INTRODUCTION

The Pendle district of East Lancashire is dominated by the celebrated landmark of Pendle Hill, but the area also offers a much wider variety of scenery. Outside of the towns of Colne and Nelson is a wealth of charming country-side liberally dotted with pleasant villages, pocket moors and woodland. The area effectively shelters between the great whaleback of Pendle Hill in the west and the main Pennine backbone in the east. Aside from Pendle itself, open country is found on Boulsworth Hill, Weets Hill and an assortment of colourful moorlands, while numerous sizeable streams such as Pendle Water and Sabden Brook offer charming strolls. Several walks also encounter the popular towpath of the Leeds-Liverpool Canal.

Villages such as Barley, Roughlee and Newchurch repose in the folds of Pendle's lap, the likes of Kelbrook, Barnoldswick and Foulridge occupy a shallow valley further east, while Trawden and lovely Wycoller back onto the higher Pennines. Pendle Forest was established as an 11th century hunting forest covering the country south from the hill towards Colne, while the name of Trawden Forest similarly survives on the other side of Colne. While the modern-day Forest of Bowland Area of Outstanding Natural Beauty is based on that great upland mass to the west, a detached section takes in the environs of Pendle Hill: as a result, many of these walks step through the AONB.

Pendle Hill is forever associated with the sinister events of 1612, glamorised into the classic witch story of the north. It began with a young girl suspected of foul play, quickly spread to her family, and resulted in an extended group being taken to Lancaster for trial and subsequent hanging. The very names of the supposed ringleaders strike a chill on a mist-wreathed day on Pendle: the surprise catch among the likes of Old Demdike and Old Chattox was the seemingly respectable Alice Nutter of Roughlee Hall. The hill has for centuries also been a beacon site, when a chain of fires would warn of approaching danger.

Whilst the route description should be sufficient to guide you around each walk, a map is recommended for greater information: Ordnance Survey 1:25,000 scale maps give the finest detail, and Explorer OL21 covers all but one of the walks, which overlaps onto Explorer 287. Many of the walks can be accessed by public transport, so where possible consider the local bus to help ease congestion.

Pendle Hill from Lower Black Moss

USEFUL INFORMATION

·Discover Pendle, Boundary Mill, Colne (01282-856186)
·Pendle Heritage Centre, Barrowford (01282-667150)
·Barnoldswick Information Centre (01282-666704)
·Open Access (0845-100 3298) www.countrysideaccess.gov.uk
·Traveline - public transport information (0870-6082608)

AROUND PENDLE

20 Short Scenic Walks

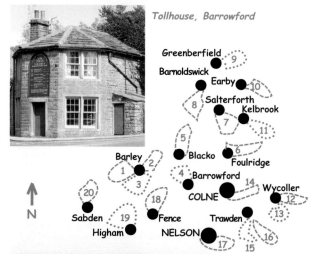

Tollhouse, Barrowford

Greenberfield 9

Barnoldswick

Earby 10

Salterforth

8 Kelbrook

7

5

Barley Blacko 6

1 2 Foulridge

3 4 Barrowford

20 COLNE 14 Wycoller

↑ 18 12

N 13

Sabden 19 Fence Trawden

Higham NELSON 16

17 15

Packhorse bridge, Wycoller

16	Walk numbers
●	Start points

A RECORD OF YOUR WALKS

WALK	DATE	NOTES
1		
2		
3		
4		
5		
6		
7		
8		
9		
10		
11		
12		
13		
14		
15		
16		
17		
18		
19		
20		

*4½ miles
from Barley*

The classic ascent of Pendle Hill from the village in its lap: a bracing stride, and a must!

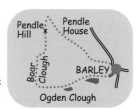

Pendle Hill
Pendle House
Boar Clough
BARLEY
Ogden Clough

Start Village centre (GR: 822403), car park
Map OS Explorer OL21, South Pennines (or OL41)
Access Long-established Pendle Way concession paths

For a note on Barley see page 10. From the car park entrance turn right over the road bridge then cross to a side road past the village hall at Barley Green: alongside is imposing Barley Green Farm-house. Past the old Nelson waterworks filter house the road runs into Ogden Clough to rise to Lower Ogden Reservoir. Losing its surface it continues the length of the reservoir. Spence Moor rises above the upper dam, while Pendle Hill's moorland slopes look impressive. Two right forks are ignored as you forge on into the upper dale past small plantations. At the end pass through a gate/stile for a stony pull up the right side of the dam of Upper Ogden Reservoir. A foot-path takes over along its northern shore, crossing a boundary wall at a kissing-gate to resume outside. Here begins a super walk along the floor of the clough immediately beyond the reservoir head.

Beyond a kissing-gate in a descending wall the moor proper is reached amid much bracken. Here the path climbs right a little before contouring on to approach Boar Clough. Ford it and ignore a short-cut to the right. Just a little further, turn right up a very easily missed, initially thin path. During a short, steep pull it becomes clearer and eases out to meet the direct path on the rim of the clough. The local name Whinberry Clough will be seen to be very apt, whinberry being another name for bilberry. Now amid wilder, open moorland, this super path rises ever gradually to approach the now insignificant clough. The stream is soon forded, and a little further the path bears away right with a feeder.

Regular cairns confirm the clear route, whose gradients remain gentle. Views open out left to Longridge, Parlick and Fair Snape Fells. The path runs to just short of the eastern scarp, merging with one from the right and rising past a sprawling cairn. By now the edge is only yards away, and the final, short pull can be savoured with a dramatic eastern view over this steep plunge. The OS column at 1893ft/577m quickly appears, and the climb is over. A perch on the rim of the mighty drop enjoys a bird's-eye view over Barley in its fold of the hills. Pendle's isolation ensures extensive views in all directions, with the South and West Pennine moors beyond the East Lancashire conurbations, and a long Dales line-up to the north.

Leave by following the path north to a wall. Don't cross but turn briefly right for the main path to commence this side of a wall-stile. This strengthened path doubles back down to a gate at the foot of the fell. Through it, slant behind Pendle House to a kissing-gate from where the path descends the fieldside to another. Bear right down the next field to a kissing-gate part way down, and a firmer path runs to another in a wall above Brown House. Go left down to one onto a drive, and go right on this past the house. As the drive goes left into a field go straight ahead to a lovely streamside path. Largely enclosed, the stream is twice crossed before emerging onto a lane. Go briefly left, then at a bend take a footbridge on the right. Turn down the final field as Barley's roofs appear ahead. At the far corner a footbridge is crossed before the path becomes enclosed for the final steps onto the main street.

Looking east from Pendle Hill

9

*3³⁄₄ miles
from Barley*

**Good views of Pendle Hill's
environs from the
quieter side of Barley**

*Start Village centre (GR: 822403), car park
Map OS Explorer OL21, South Pennines (or OL41)*

Barley is an unassuming village cradled by Pendle Hill, with the Pendle Inn, a restaurant, tearooms and WCs. An information centre at the car park is open in season and winter weekends, also serving refreshments. The car park occupies the site of an old mill dam, for being near the larger settlements the village was caught up in the Industrial Revolution: cotton factories and earlier small scale handloom-weaving meant this was a busy little spot.

From the car park head right on the main street past the pub, and when the road swings sharp left out of the village, go straight ahead on a private access road. This rises to the dam of Lower Black Moss Reservoir, then runs along the shore. Dating from 1903, it is a good foreground to the classic profile of Pendle Hill. Beyond it a rough track takes over: fork right up to the dam of Upper Black Moss Reservoir (1894), and resume outside its bank. At the end the improved track crosses the inflow and rises by the stream onto a road at Black Moss. Cross over and up Mountain farm drive. When it swings away to a cattle-grid, keep on up the stream-side to a stile at the end. Don't use it but take one in the corner to your right, and head away with a new hedge. When it turns up towards the farm, keep straight on to rejoin the drive: in front is a wall-stile from where cross to a stile into a wooded gill. Drop to a footbridge and a stile back out, then ascend the reedy pasture with a fence. At the top go right a few yards to a stile in the wall, trading Pendle Hill for Boulsworth Hill in your extensive view. Drop down to a wall-stile onto a road and go briefly right to a junction.

A few yards along the side road take a gate on the left to drop right to a stile onto a drive at a lone house. Cross straight over to a small gate and slant down to a wall-stile. Now rise to a wall corner and follow the wall up to a ruin. Here rise right to a wall-stile on the skyline ahead, and bear right from it, briefly, to an old gateway onto a back road. A gate opposite admits to the tame Stang Top Moor, and a track heads away, passing beneath an OS column above an old quarry. Remain with the fence on your left as the track fades, commencing a long slant down the big pasture. As the fence turns off, maintain your slant to approach the bottom corner. From a bridle-gate a path descends through new plantings to another such gate in the bottom corner. Enclosed by greenery it descends with a stream to White Hough Outdoor Education Centre.

Continue down the drive to the hamlet of White Hough: on the left amid this colourful cluster is White Hough Farm, a hugely attractive old house with mullioned and transomed windows. Just beyond, as the road swings sharp left in front of the stream, take a broad track right. This is the old road to Barley, and runs upstream in grand surrounds to Narrowgates. Two attractive rows of weavers' cottages precede the remains of a cotton mill closed in the 1960s: note the preserved square chimney. Just beyond the old mill, a path goes forward to re-enter the car park.

Narrowgates

11

4 miles from Barley

Stunning Pendle views in the heart of Witch Country

Start Village centre (GR: 822403), car park
Map OS Explorer OL21, South Pennines (or OL41)

For a note on Barley see page 10. From the car park entrance turn right over the bridge then cross to a side road past the village hall at Barley Green. Alongside is imposing Barley Green Farmhouse as the road runs on past a 1912 filter house into Ogden Clough. Rising to the dam of Lower Ogden Reservoir (completed 1914) the road loses its surface and continues along its length. Spence Moor rises above the upper dam, while Pendle Hill's immediate moorland slopes look suitably impressive. Two right forks are ignored as you forge on into the upper dale beneath small plantations. At the end pass through a gate/stile for a stony pull up the right side of the dam to the foot of Upper Ogden Reservoir, opened in 1906.

Turn on the dam top to a stile onto the foot of rough moorland. A path ascends moist, reedy terrain to join a crumbling wall to the left. Look back to a superb profile of Pendle's eastern scarp beyond the reservoir, and also into the recesses of Ogden Clough beneath Spence Moor. Four sheets of water are now in view as the Black Moss twosome beyond Barley appear, while on a clear day Penyghent is joined by Buckden Pike and Great Whernside. The wall is traced up to the brow on Driver Height, the latter, drier stages largely pathless. At 1230ft/375m this high point of the walk merits a repose on a grassy patch. Ahead is the linear sprawl of the East Lancashire towns beneath the South Pennine moors.

An immediate descent with the wall emerges into a large, sloping pasture to drop steeply to a gate onto narrow Well Head Road. Turn left on this to Newchurch. A little before the village is Faughs Quarry, where heather-draped rocks feature an intriguing carving: one of the Pendle Witches is said to have met the devil here.... Advance on past the church to a central junction. St Mary's church tower dates from 1544: near the porch is the 'witch's grave', reputedly that of Alice Nutter. Also in this tiny hillside village are WCs by the old slaughter-house, and 'Witches Galore', a unique shop. Missing is the Lamb Inn at the junction, which sadly called a final last orders a couple of decades ago. Keep left up the main street, past the houses to a bend at the top. Mighty Pendle is revealed in all its glory, with Barley nestling below.

Turn right here along a drive, but leave almost at once by a small gate in front, following the wall along the broad ridge-top outside the wood. Keen eyes will pick out the flat top of Ingleborough on the skyline above Barley. Part way along an old wall-stile admits into the trees, and a slanting path cuts a corner of the wood to a stile at the end. Emerging reveals big views over the environs of Roughlee and Blacko. Head away to rejoin the ridge-wall on the left, and follow this down Thorny Bank outside another plantation. On reaching a corner-stile past an intervening one, a little path follows the other side of the wall down the colourful, broad ridge-end to a stile onto an enclosed track. Turn left on this inviting way, which runs into woodland and on above Boothman Wood to emerge with Pendle providing a final, memorable flourish. Below is a glimpse of the old mill chimney at Narrowgates. The track drops stonily down into the village by way of cottages at Bridge End.

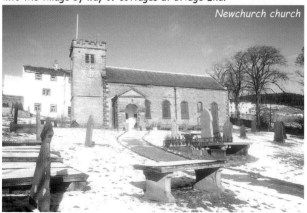

Newchurch church

3¹2 miles from Barrowford

Lots of interest as a nice old village sits between big views and a streamside return

Start Pendle Heritage Centre
(GR: 862397), car park
Map OS Explorer OL21, South Pennines (or OL41)

Pendle Heritage Centre is based in the splendid 17th century Park Hill, and has shop, tearoom, exhibitions, 14th century cruck barn and 18th century walled gardens. Over the bridge on the edge of this bustling village is a restored tollhouse of 1805, complete with notice of tolls. From the centre a path runs down through the park behind it, alongside Pendle Water to a footbridge. Cross this and the road and up the side of the White Bear: dating from the 17th century it has a three-storey porch and mullioned windows. Continue up past most of the housing to a sharp bend, then go straight ahead on Pasture House farm drive. Over to the right is Stansfield Tower on Blacko Hill. Half way up, beyond allotments, take a stile on the left and head off with a fence. Quickly go right over a footbridge to rise by a hedge. Higher, it becomes enclosed by trees to rise to a stile at a barn. Cross to one above and up a small enclosure to a small gate into a field. Ignoring an early stile on the left, ascend this long pasture with a line of trees on the left.

Through an old hedge-line at the top a brow is reached: advance forward to reveal a grand prospect dominated by Pendle Hill. Roughlee appears below on reaching a stile at the end, as walls replace foliage. Slant gently left down the field, and reaching a bank at the bottom, a path drops left to stepping-stones on Pendle Water. Behind, the road is joined at a stile. Go briefly left into Roughlee, where the Bay Horse pub stands by the bridge. Return along the front of a row of white cottages, immediately off a junction just short of the pub. This narrows to run along the front of Roughlee Old Hall, a superb house with mullioned windows and a

1536 datestone from an earlier building. It was reputedly home of Alice Nutter, a 'lady' among the clutch of Pendle Witches.

Turn up the drive at the end, through Hollin Farm and on to a house at Middlewood. Through a kissing-gate at the end advance on the field by an overgrown way. Through a stile at the end resume with a fence, dropping to a small gate onto a road behind a barn. From one almost opposite head away on a wooded bank above Pendle Water. Just short of the top take a path right to run through open terrain above the stream: keeping right at a fork the path runs closer to it. By the water's edge at a marshy bend a path partly escapes through higher reeds, maintaining height to run to a stile in a hedge ahead. The way keeps this height above a wooded bank, opening out to descend open pasture towards Water Meetings. Bear left to a footbridge on Blacko Water and turn downstream on a forming track to arrive at the lovely confluence, where it merges into Pendle Water. The track runs on to a gate onto an access road at a bridge.

Across the bridge turn downstream for a grand walk to Higherford, en route passing an old weir beyond isolated Old Oak Tree Cottage. At the end you join residential Barleydale Road: keep on to the historic Higherford Bridge just round the corner. Cross this to cobbled Pinfold and onto the main road at a church. Cross the road and turn right past the Old Bridge pub. Don't cross the road bridge at this busy corner: for the last lap, take a path alongside it to trace the wooded stream back to the start.

Roughlee Old Hall

15

3¹2 miles from Blacko

**Lovely streamside walking
in a quiet corner of Pendle**

*Start Blacko Foot (GR: 849414),
parking area off A682
Map OS Explorer OL21,
South Pennines (or OL41)*

From a few steps by the bridge a path heads upstream with lively Blacko Water. Through a stile at the end, ignore a foot-bridge and advance to another stile, then cross a pasture into trees to steps up onto a road. Cross the bridge and descend steps to a footbridge over a slab bridge at a confluence. Over the side-stream, follow the main stream, now Admergill Water, on a thin path through several pastures linked by stiles. Approaching the hamlet of Lower Admergill, cross a footbridge on the stream and resume to a gate into the grounds of the first house. Go right on the drive over a cattle-grid and bridge to join another drive, then left on this the short way to Admergill Hall Farm, a splendid 17th century house with leaning mullioned windows, some arch-headed.

Keep straight on the drive until it turns up to the left: Burn Moor rises high above. Through a gate/stile in front continue upstream, through a pleasant pasture to a stile by the right-hand of two gates. A continuing path runs through a meadow to a stile at the end accessing a slab bridge. From it a grand little path climbs steeply away through a bank of newly-planted trees, with super views over the upper reaches of this side valley. Near the top the path slants across to a stile onto the A682: just along to the left is the Moorcock Inn. From a stile opposite, a path slants left up to a wall with a farm at Admergill Pasture behind. Here double back right with the wall: Stansfield Tower is straight ahead, Burn Moor rises across Admergill, and Pendle Hill is also fully revealed. At the wall-end, slant across the large field well above an isolated stone wall: this is a good example of a bield (sheep shelter). A stile in the opposite wall will not be located until upon it just above a kink, whence cross the flat pasture to the far corner. Stansfield Tower on Blacko Hill, built around 1890, is now at its nearest point. Down to the left are the Foulridge Reservoirs backed by Kelbrook Moor.

From a corner stile drop right with a line of hawthorns pointing to Blacko Hill Side. Ahead is a big sweep of East Lancashire backed by the South Pennines. A stile puts you between the buildings, where turn right along the front of the houses and out on the drive. This turns to descend by a line of hollies to emerge by modern housing onto a road at Blacko. Turn briefly right, then left down a cul-de-sac, Malkin Close. A path slopes off right to emerge between houses onto the A682. Along to the left is the Rising Sun pub.

Cross to a gate almost opposite, then over the field to a corner gateway. Continue away with a hedge on your right, but part way on bear left with a line of trees to shadow a wooded gill down to a wall-stile. A pleasant path descends a colourful pasture to a wall-stile at the bottom. Don't go left to the farm bridge, but turn right on a track to Water Meetings, a minute or so upstream. At this lovely spot Blacko Water merges into Pendle Water, and in days past this was a popular local stroll and picnic spot. The track fades as you trace the right branch upstream to a footbridge just ahead. Across, bear right up the steep bank to a tiny gate in the skyline fence. Head away to a stile ahead, then simply follow the fieldside all the way along to Blacko Foot, passing left of the buildings and out onto the road. The start point is just down to the right.

Admergill Hall

17

4³4 miles from Foulridge

**Colourful, gentle hills
offering wide panoramas**

*Start Foulridge Wharf
(GR: 888426), car park*

Map OS Explorer OL21, South Pennines

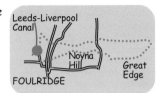

Foulridge is a small village with several pubs and shops. The Wharf was an integral part of the Leeds-Liverpool Canal's hey-day: note the paintwork on the surviving warehouse. The moorings host a colourful array of boats, with public cruises and a tearoom. Here the canal enters the mile-long Foulridge Tunnel. From the Wharf head back up the road: on meeting a through road go left on Cromwell Street to an attractive green. At the end climb steps to the main road and cross to ascend a narrow lane. At the top go right a few yards, then left up a corner of a tiny green. Advance just a few yards up this back road, and take a snicket on the left between houses. This runs from gardens to emerge into a field. Bear left on a straight line through several fields: after a couple of gates is a corner wall-stile, and from a gateway in the next wall, rise left to a bridle-gate on the brow. Excellent views look to an array of Yorkshire Dales heights dominated by Ingleborough.

Turn right to ascend with the wall, with a shapely knoll above. The path contours round its left side and across the field to a wall-stile. Through this ascend the wallside, meeting one further stile onto Noyna Hill's broad top. Pendle Hill looms large over Burn Moor across the valley. A slight rise follows an intervening stile, then take a small gate on the right. A path runs enclosed for 50 yards to a brow. Emerging, slant left down to a stile, then down to a tiny corner gate onto Cob Lane at Noyna End. Opposite the house, take a gate on the left. A grassy track doubles back across the field, but is left within a hundred yards by turning right down to a footbridge. A path runs downstream towards a wall: don't pass through the gate but turn steeply up the near side to a stile in the wall at the top.

Continue rising with a fence up the extensive reedy tract of Great Edge, pausing to look back over Foulridge reservoirs, with Pendle Hill and Bowland's moors leading round to Yorkshire's Three Peaks.

At the top veer right to a ladder-stile in the wall. Head away with a wall as far as a stile in it just short of its high point. Cross the field centre to a stile opposite, then advance past greenery to a wall-stile. Bear left to a farm track, following it through a gate and across to a corner with Kelbrook Moor over the wall. Don't enter but go left down the wallside to a corner gate into a walled way. Moist until opening out, stay with the right-hand wall down to a farm road. Continue down, absorbing a drive, and onto Cob Lane. Go briefly left then take an enclosed green way right. Emerging into a field a faint way drops to a bridle-gate, resuming above a wall to Ambwell. Pass the house and continue to a bridle-gate at the far end. Retain this course across a field, dropping all the while, through a gateway to a gate/stile just beyond. A little path traces the right-hand wall beneath a scrubby bank down to a gate/stile onto a drive, with a back road just below. Go briefly left and take a gate on the right at a big house, Cragg Farm. Drop to a gate just beneath it, from where a cart track descends to the A56. Cross to a gate/stile opposite and slant right down the field, in the corner using an old crossing of the former railway. A grassy way drops into a field, then advance to a footbridge. A path heads away, rising to a canal bridge. Join the towpath and go left, the waterway leading quickly back to the wharf.

On Noyna Hill

3¾ miles from Salterforth

Low-level walking with the towpath among numerous interesting features

Start Anchor Inn
(GR: 887453), Salterforth
Moorings car park opposite
Map OS Explorer OL21, South Pennines

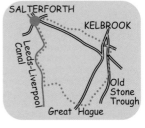

SALTERFORTH
KELBROOK
Leeds-Liverpool Canal
Old Stone Trough
Great Hague

The Anchor is a celebrated canalside pub astride an old salt way, in use in packhorse times: its cellar features stalactite formations as a result of its damp situation beneath the canal. Join the towpath alongside it and head off south through charming rural surroundings. Features of interest include a milestone (Liverpool 84, Leeds 43¼), colourful moorings opposite and views across to Kelbrook Moor. Pass beneath the first stone-arched bridge and on to Mill Hill Bridge a little further: this shelters the next milestone. Under it leave by steps on the left, and without crossing the bridge pass through a gate and bear left down the field to a footbridge on a drain near the corner. Bear right across a large flat pasture, aiming for the farm at Great Hague on the brow. From a gate/stile near the corner an enclosed track ascends to the farm. En route you cross the old Skipton-Colne railway: this once vital Yorkshire-Lancashire link closed in 1970. Ascending into the yard bear right at the top to emerge past the splendid old house onto the A56.

Turn briefly right on the footway and cross to a stile. Ascend the field to a wall above, but instead of passing through go left with it to a footbridge on a tree-lined stream, then cross to a gate/stile. Keep on to the rear of a house, using a concessionary path into its garden. Turn right on the drive out past attractive dwellings to emerge onto Old Stone Trough Lane at Old Stone Trough. A nice rows of cottages stand on the left, while a spring falls into the trough itself on the right. Go left for a few minutes to the edge of Kelbrook. Just after Cob Lane comes in on the right at Yellow Hall, the road swings left downhill: here go right to a stile set back across a grass sward. An enclosed path heads away between fields, and a stile at the end sends you down a fieldside. Through a stile at the bottom you emerge onto a back road at Low Fold. Go left on the beckside road to the junction with Main Street. To the right is the church of St Mary the Virgin, dating from 1839.

Advance straight on Vicarage Road to the main road ahead. If you're here on Saturday lunch there's a chippy to the left. Cross straight over to a rough road alongside the Craven Heifer pub. Passing a house a walled footway takes over. Ending at a small gate into a field, head away with a hedge on the right. A stile at the end sends stone steps down onto a railway cutting: bear right a few yards and then out the other side. Head away down a fenceside to a stone-slab footbridge on a larger drain, quickly becoming a broader, embanked grass track as you merge with the hedge on your right. Tapering at the end alongside the Barnoldswick road, pass through a kissing-gate to commence a splendid stroll by a watercourse all the way back to Salterforth. It later becomes enclosed then runs by an old factory car park before emerging onto the road: cross a little further along and turn up Salterforth Lane back to the start.

The canal south of Salterforth

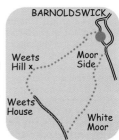

4¾ miles from Barnoldswick

A bracing ascent of a Pendle landmark with a moorland return

Start Bancroft Mill (GR: 874461), roadside parking
Map OS Explorer OL21, South Pennines (or OL41)

Locally 'Barlick', this independent little town boasts a wide range of services: Town Square is an attractive focal point. Bancroft Mill with its circular red-brick chimney is home to a rare steam engine that draws visitors when in operation on certain days during the year. From the mill turn left (towards town) briefly, then go left on suburban Moorgate Road. This quickly leaves modern suburbia and continues as Folly Lane, soon zigzagging steeply uphill. A pause is merited to look back over town backed by a wide sweep of Dales hills. A little past Standridge Farm, take a gate/stile on the right and resume up the fieldside. This grand stride maintains its course when the parallel lane turns off. Continue uphill all the way with a wall to the left, through several stiles as the terrain changes to rougher grassy moorland above a colourful steep bank.

The steeper work is accomplished to leave a very gentle stride, and through the final stile a crumbling pillar overlooks a small ravine. All of this stage enjoys fine panoramic views west to Bowland and north across lowland Craven to the Yorkshire Dales dominated by Ingleborough and Penyghent. While a path remains with the wall over the flat top of Weets Hill, an early right fork runs past a scrappy cairn to the Ordnance Survey column at 1302ft/397m. The already fine views are now enhanced by the inclusion of Pendle Hill looming impressively close, with Longridge Fell behind. Northwards is a classic English landscape, with the tree-lined green fields of the Ribble Valley leading the eye to the Bowland moors and the peaks of the Yorkshire Dales.

Another path returns to the wall to drop onto Gisburn Old Road at a gate off the hill. This was a packhorse route prior to construction of the turnpike below - the present A682. A short-lived way runs to isolated Weets House, and its drive leads out. Follow this cul-de-sac road for almost a mile past several houses: in a wide panorama of East Lancashire, Boulsworth Hill leads round to the moors above Burnley, while further right are Admergill and Burn Moor backed by Pendle. Just before the isolated Peel's House take a gate on the left just beyond an earlier signed path.

Head away on a wallside track to the terminus of Lister Well Road, a walled green lane. Below are Foulridge reservoirs, with Elslack Moor, Kelbrook Moor and Great Edge ahead. This provides a gem of a stroll alongside heathery White Moor. The way remains a classic as heather moorland rapidly envelops your way, even down to its verges. The way gradually declines until commencing a more pronounced descent. After absorbing Prospect Farm drive, drop a little lower to a bend then take a gate/stile on the left. Entering a tract of heather moor a level little path heads away. Approaching a few reeds in the centre bear right, maintaining a level course over a tiny stream before dropping right to a wall below, just yards on from an outer corner. Double back a few yards to the corner and a wallside path drops to a stile at the bottom. Through it take a gate just behind and down onto the drive at Moor Side, following it down to the B6251 Barnoldswick-Foulridge road. Go left and left again on Gillians Lane which leads quickly back to the start.

Pendle Hill from Weets Hill

*3¹/4 miles
from Greenberfield*

**A low-level stroll with
towpath features and
two lovely old churches**

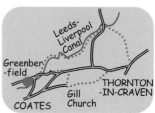

*Start Greenberfield Locks
(GR: 887481), car park off Barnoldswick-Thornton road
Map OS Explorer OL21, South Pennines*

     The Leeds-Liverpool Canal runs a 127¹/4-mile course, most northerly of three trans-Pennine waterways. Rather than tunnelling below the hills, this took advantage of the Aire Gap to breach the Pennines with a chain of locks. Begun in 1770 and fully opened in 1816 for what proved to be a short-lived industrial use, today it is a vibrant leisure amenity for walkers, bargees, anglers, naturalists and cyclists. Greenberfield Locks are a set of three that lift the canal to its highest altitude: a red-brick water supply house of 1893, boaters' facilities, and a refreshment kiosk add to the colour and interest. Join the towpath and head left (north) only as far as the road bridge after the first lock. Here join the road, cross the bridge and follow the road to the B6252. Initially you need not join it as a good path runs on the wooded bank to your left.

     Go briefly left towards the Rolls-Royce factory and cross to a kissing-gate just before a 'Welcome to Barnoldswick' sign. A little path rises past Gill Hall. Turn to look back at its front with an array of mullioned windows: dating from the 16th century, it was once the rectory. Continue on the fieldside above the wooded cleft of The Gill, and at the top a stile admits into St Mary-le-Gill churchyard. Pass to the right to the front of the church and a gateway onto its access road. This splendid old church (also known as Gill Church) has a large 16th century tower and an incredibly vast 500 year-old roof, while its lovely interior features a fine arrangement of box-pews and an awesome three-decker pulpit.

From the gateway go left down a narrow snicket between churchyard and cemetery. This descends to a slab crossing of the stream and up onto Ghyll golf course. Rise left of a small plantation and up again to a path through a belt of trees to a kissing-gate off the course. Rise away, skirting a grassy knoll and aiming for Thornton church tower. This modest elevation gives sweeping views north to a Dales skyline from Ingleborough to Great Whernside: behind you are the Bowland moors. Cross an access track and a stile and on to a stile at the end onto the bank above the B6252. Go right, following the verge to a stile in the hedge to cross to the largely 15th century St Mary's church. Opposite is Thornton Hall Farm country park.

Go right past charming almshouses of 1815, and along the footway to a junction with the A56 at Thornton Hill. Turn left into the village centre, with stocks on a green. At the first junction go left on an access road leaving the village to rise to a brow. Descend past Shed Laithe and on between fields, as far as a small gate on the left. Leave the drive and cross to a slab footbridge leading to a tidy ascent of Castleber Hill, a grassy knoll with a fine panorama. Drop down to the canal at your feet, a gate accesses the towpath. Turn left, under South Field Bridge for a relaxing stroll through rolling West Craven countryside back to the start, as the canal meanders around grassy knolls formed at the end of the Ice Age.

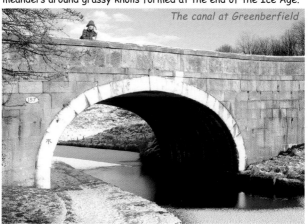

The canal at Greenberfield

4¹⁄₄ miles from Earby

Bracing strides on fine old ways between heather moors

Start Village centre (GR: 907468), Victoria Road car park
Map OS Explorer OL21, South Pennines

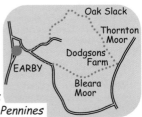

Earby is a sizeable village with shops, pubs and café. Housed in a 400-year old grammar school is the Museum of Yorkshire Dales Lead Mining. From a mini-roundabout at the end of Victoria Road, just past the bus stops turn right, past the Coronation Hall of 1911, now a library. Just past here bear left on Water Street: bridging the stream it becomes Red Lion Street and passes the eponymous pub. It continues as Moor Brow Road, then Birch Hall Lane, and at a corner reaches the youth hostel. Glen Cottage has served thousands of walkers since 1955, many detouring from the Pennine Way.

Immediately after it take a track left, but leave quickly as a stile on the left sends a path down to a footbridge in trees. Steps slant right up the other side to emerge in a field. Rise away, joining a hedge to reach a stile onto an enclosed track, Gaylands Lane. From a stile opposite turn to shadow the lane up the field, veering slightly off to a fence-stile ahead. Now bear more left and along a brow to a stile in the wall rising left. A thin path heads away to meet an old sunken way: turn right with this to the top to find a solid cairn and a seat. By this stage you have a magnificent panorama, including Yorkshire's Three Peaks and a full Bowland skyline. As the sunken way ends pass through the nearest gateway and along a fainter grassy way with an old wall on the right. Meeting an access road above Thornton Highgate, pass through the gate on your right then left over the cattle-grid to follow the access road down to Oak Slack: ahead is a good spread of Thornton and Bleara Moors.

Don't enter the farm but drop right to a corner stile and on through a gateway. Bear right down the field to a farm bridge on tree-lined Wentcliff Brook, before the corner. Through a gate the track forks: go right over a sidestream and up a few yards to another gate. Rise left up the fieldside, a grand old grassy way shadowing the tree-lined clough. Through a gate/stile at the top it becomes enclosed to drop left over the stream to an abandoned farmhouse. Pass through the gate behind and rise away on a nice line above the stream. Continue up to the top corner, where a gate/stile put you in another pasture top at the head of the stream, with heathery Thornton Moor just above. Pendle's great whaleback rises beyond Weets Hill. Cross to another gate just ahead from where a splendid green way, Dodgson Lane, rises between walls to Dodgsons Farm.

Continue straight up the access road to a brow yards short of a road. Just before the brow take a gate on the right, and a track follows a wall away. Through a corner gate an enclosed section leads on to open out, remaining with the left-hand wall to drop steadily to the scant ruins of Higher Verjuice Bank. With heathery Bleara Moor over the wall, remain on this improving green way (Stanridge Clough Lane) down the edge of the pasture, all the way to a bridle-gate at the bottom. A sunken continuation between walls drops to a bend where a farm track takes over: from a stile in front head down the field, merging with the right-hand wall to drop to a gate/stile at the bottom. A short enclosed path drops past trees and slants right to a house, following the drive left onto Coolham Lane. Turn right into the edge of Earby, keeping straight on to finish.

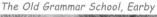

The Old Grammar School, Earby

4¾ miles from Kelbrook

Rolling hills and heather moors

Start Village centre
(GR: 902447), roadside parking
Map OS Explorer OL21,
South Pennines

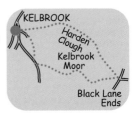

Leave on Vicarage Road opposite the Craven Heifer, onto Main Street with St Mary's church to your left. Follow a side road ahead with the beck on your left: as it swings right take a left branch over the beck. A little further, on the village edge, ignore paths either way and advance on Heads Lane. Kelbrook Moor rises to the right across the valley of Harden Beck. The road ends at Heads House Farm, and a cart track rises to a covered reservoir. From a gate/stile in front ascend the fieldside to a gate. Continue on the fading sunken way up a field centre, and on through two gates. Keep right of a ditch, past a wall corner to a gate/stile in a corner just beyond. Advance to cross a tiny stream then leave the ascending wall and contour right to a stile in a facing wall above the tree-lined beck.

A trod crosses rough pasture to a gate, with a footbridge on the stream ahead. Across it the path rises, swinging left to a house at Harden Clough. A gate/stile admits to its garden, passing left of the house and down to a gate onto its drive at the bottom. Across a footbridge a path slants up a steep, colourful bank above: Kelbrook Wood decorates Kelbrook Moor's nearby flank. Above a wall-stile the path rises to Scald Bank. Pass above the house, up a track to join its ascending drive. As it swings left cross to a wall-stile ahead, and cross rough pasture to the left of the brow ahead. Rise by the wall to a gate above: Black Lane Ends appears, with Cowling's Earl Crag beyond. Descend the wallside to the buildings, and a gate into the car park. The Black Lane Ends pub is the heart of this isolated community on the old Skipton-Colne turnpike road.

Back in the field behind the pub rise left to a stile in the wall. A path crosses reeds to another stile from where you cross the dome of Piked Edge: a few rocks sit to the right. Views look to

Boulsworth Hill, Pendle Hill, Ingleborough, Penyghent, Buckden Pike and Great Whernside. Aiming for Copy House, drop to a stile in the far corner. A clear way crosses a field centre to a stile, then follow the wall to the farm. From a stile onto its drive advance past the house and on a grass track through a tapering enclosure. A gate at the end puts you into a field corner, advance a few strides to a gate/stile on the right onto Kelbrook Moor. Head away, a reedy track aims for the top of a cluster of trees. On the right, slopes rise to the moor summit. The track fades but a heathery stride leads to a second stand of trees. Stunning views look to a Bowland skyline between Pendle and Ingleborough. Beyond the trees bear left down the moor to a corner where fence and wall meet, though being on Open Access land you might be drawn by a clearer path running to a small gateway in the wall ahead, which could be followed to the bottom corner.

Through the gateway resume down heathery Roger Moor, a little above the wall to avoid moistness. Approaching a farm over the wall, don't follow faithfully but contour right through an old quarry. This avoids a cul-de-sac corner to find another wall corner in front. From it follow the wall a little further down to a ladder-stile in a small corner. Leave the moor and descend to a stile onto Cob Lane at a farm road junction. Turn down for a minute, then take a drive right past a house: a path runs outside the garden into a field. Drop to the wall heading away, using a stile to resume on the other side of stream and fence. The tiny stream sinks underground at the bottom: bear right to a gate/stile and descend again, past the re-born stream to a gate/stile in front of houses below. Bear left down the road back to the start. *Pendle Hill from Kelbrook Moor*

3¾ miles from Wycoller

**A fascinating exploration
of Wycoller's little valley
and its colourful flanks**

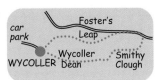

Start **Village centre (GR: 931393), car park on access road**
Map **OS Explorer OL21, South Pennines**

Wycoller is an absorbing hamlet by-passed by the outside world since the Industrial Revolution failed to gain a foothold. It is difficult to believe that two centuries ago, several hundred people lived here. Handloom weaving was a major industry, but as the large mills sprang up, workers abandoned the place to take employment in the towns. As a result Wycoller spent much of the 20th century largely derelict, but its very isolation and character have ensured its popularity at the heart of a country park. Central are the ruins of 16th century Wycoller Hall, thought to have been the Ferndean Manor of Charlotte Bronte's 'Jane Eyre'. Alongside is an ancient clapper bridge, while a characterful packhorse bridge stands by a ford. Restored Aisled Barn was built in the 1630s to store grain, and has displays of local interest. There is a tearoom/craft centre.

Cross the packhorse bridge to the hall and ascend steps up the grassy bank behind. At the top a broad, enclosed path rises away, and Pendle Hill is seen back to the left. Upright slabs by the path are a good example of vaccary walling - a vaccary was a cattle farm. Approaching a sunken section, take a gate/stile on the right and cross a field to a stile: above is the Atom Panopticon, a modern sculpture. The little path rises very gently beneath it, through a couple of vaccary walls to a fork: keep straight on above the fence, through further vaccary walls. Massive views look across Wycoller Dean to Boulsworth Hill, while just ahead are the rocks of Foster's Leap. After the next stile the path forks, and ignoring the thin way rising left, keep on to where a higher path merges and on to a bridle-gate in the wall ahead. The path drops slightly to the next one, and on to another in front of the first of two houses ahead. Turn up the steep drive beneath a wood as far as a hairpin bend left. Just yards higher an old grassy way contours off to the right beneath the scattered lower rocks of Foster's Leap. Remaining level it fades somewhat, but keep straight on beneath a steeper bank, rising very slightly then a little more to a house that appears ahead at Higher Key Stiles: a wall-stile gives access. Pass along the front and out on the driveway past another old house and up onto a road.

Turn right for half a mile as the road traverses the edge of moorland. Ahead is Watersheddles Reservoir, with Wolf Stones on the left skyline. After the last house it swings sharply left, just past which turn down an initially enclosed byway into the head of Smithy Clough. The rough road runs unfailingly down, crossing the stream by a stone-arched bridge amid the hummocks of Smithy Clough Scar, also known as Hilly Holes. These hushings result from centuries-old limestone extraction, where water released from dams scoured vegetation away. Views stretch far over Pendle country to the big hill itself. The track swings up to a brow and path junction where Bronte Way and Pendle Way meet. Pass through a gate/stile on the right and descend the track to Parson Lee Farm. Its drive merges with another at a confluence, to resume as a traffic-free byway with the stream. This happy arrangement is maintained through Wycoller Dean back to the start, passing Copy House foot-bridge and the historic, single-slab Clam Bridge alongside a ford.

Foster's Leap, looking over Wycoller Dean to Boulsworth Hill

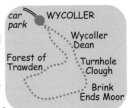

4¼ miles from Wycoller

A colourful clough and moorland in an ancient hunting forest

Start Village centre (GR: 931393), car park on access road   *Map* OS Explorer OL21, South Pennines

Cross the packhorse bridge on Wycoller Beck to the ruins of the hall, and follow the main access road to its right past Aisled Barn out of the hamlet. A delightful streamside course leads past the historic, single-slab Clam Bridge at a ford, and also Copy House footbridge. Reaching a fork at a confluence ignore both farm drives heading away, and from a kissing-gate resume on a beckside path to start a lovely walk through Turnhole Clough. Briefly faint, it quickly crosses a footbridge to resume on the other bank. Soon reaching another footbridge via a kissing-gate, don't cross but take a super woodland path on your own bank. This rises away to a kissing-gate out at the far corner: resume outside the trees, with bracken flanks leading to rock outcrops above. Ahead are Boulsworth Hill's moorland slopes. When the fence drops away keep on through a bridle-gate by the beck and rise grandly across bracken-covered flanks to a gate onto Brink Ends Moor. Here you meet a bridleway at an old boundary stone. Keep right on the path rising gently through colourful terrain above the deep clough. The contours of Boulsworth Hill now entirely dominate this surround of rolling moorland, while sections of stone causey testify to the history of this old packhorse route.

In the company of Saucer Hill Clough, a lengthy section with a sturdy wall leads to the brow of the hill, where Pendle Hill appears. A firm track now descends to a junction with an access road. Turn right on this over the cattle-grid off the moor and through a field. Absorbing a farm drive it drops down to become enclosed at a cottage at Mean Moss. Leave the road here, and from a small gate pass along the front of the house to a stile by wooden sheds. Resume across the field to a wall-stile, and on through two further fields with a wall close by to the left: the second has a good path through rough moor-grass. The end stile is reached with New Laith Farm across the field in front. Don't advance to it, but turn right on the wallside. Just short of the corner a stile at a large gatepost admits to a small corner of rough pasture. Go left through the gate and a walled way heads away. At the end, a grassy track advances straight on with a reedy ditch down to a gate/stile. Cross to a quality old corner stile and down a wallside to a gate/stile into rougher pasture. Follow the crumbling right-hand wall away as it curves around to a sturdy wall. Just fifty yards down this is a stile, and just below that a bridle-gate in the corner. Wycoller Dean is now revealed beneath Foster's Leap and the moorland slopes.

Descend with the wall, and stay with it as it swings left: the picture of Wycoller's valley improves throughout this section. Before the bottom corner cross at a bridle-gate, and from a stile behind, resume on a faint path down the other side past a wood. At the bottom corner go briefly left to a wall-stile, then cross to the buildings at Copy House. Pass right of the house, and as the drive heads away, take a gap-stile on the right to descend the wallside to Wycoller Beck. Either cross the small bridge to the rough road to go left and finish, or use the firm permissive path on this side, downstream by nature ponds to the clapper bridge in the hamlet.

Wycoller Hall

4 miles from Colne

Easy walking in the environs of a lively beck, visiting a characterful hilltop hamlet

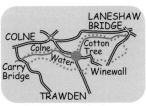

Start **Cotton Tree**
(GR: 908401), Ball Grove car park at east end of town
Map **OS Explorer OL21, South Pennines**

Ball Grove Park is a popular nature reserve: alongside is the Cotton Tree pub. From the car park follow the main track upstream with Colne Water, past a playground and an attractive pond. More open surrounds lead past a cottage and pleasantly along to a fork: while the main track rises left, go straight ahead on a grassier one to rejoin the stream at the end, at an old weir. A firm path traces it along to a restored pond (Upper Ball Grove Lodge), just past which is a footbridge on Colne Water. Across, a flagged path runs an enclosed course away from the stream to drop back down at the end to re-cross on another footbridge. An enclosed path then resumes upstream (via a footbridge on a sidestream) to a stile onto the road at Covey Bridge on the edge of Laneshaw Bridge.

Across the single-arched bridge follow the road climbing away. On levelling out take a stile on the left and head away with a wall: ahead are big views to Boulsworth Hill. Through a gate/stile at the end turn right with another wall, and remain with it to rise gently through several gates/stiles: the brow reveals Pendle Hill ahead. Reaching a house at Souteril Laith, from a gate/stile at the end a path runs by the drive out onto a road. Cross to a gate/stile and head away, soon crossing the field centre on a little path to a gate/stile opposite. This sends a part enclosed path above an old quarry to lead out onto a drive and road at Hill Top, Winewall. Turn briefly right into this lovely corner, noting the splendid old houses of Hill Top Farm and Fold Farm on your right. Opposite the latter take a short drive on the left, becoming a green way with big views over Colne backed by Pendle Hill. At the end drop right down a snicket and steps, past a house side and down onto a road. Go briefly left to the bend and keep left on a private road, Well Head. Reaching a former chapel fork right, dropping slightly and just past a small green, turn right down a short access road to a short row of houses. A surfaced path takes over at the bottom, slanting down a steep bank to emerge between terraces onto the Trawden road.

Cross and go right a short way as far as a bridge on Trawden Brook. Rise past a house to a bridle-gate, and follow a track up to fade on the brow. Just ahead take a stile on the left and rise away alongside a wall. At the top corner pass through a small gate and curve right around to another in a recess in front of a house. Immediately after it take a gate into its yard, then left to a small gate into a large sloping pasture. With Colne outspread ahead drop to the far corner, avoiding a moist spring as you approach. Through a kissing-gate join a clear path running left on the edge of woodland, emerging via a stile overlooking Colne Water. The thin path runs grandly on through open pastures, in the second rising slightly above a wooded bank to a stile onto a back road. Go right to drop down to the fine single arch of Carry Bridge. Across it turn right on Old Mill Drive, quickly deflected right on a path alongside the stream, initially in trees. Remain on the path tracing its length, pleasantly along to a wooded bank where steps take you up onto the Trawden road again. Go right on the footway to quickly finish.

Winewall, with Boulsworth Hill behind

4¹4 miles from Trawden

Richly varied terrain above Trawden's side valley

Start Village centre
(GR: 911386), roadside parking
Map OS Explorer OL21,
South Pennines

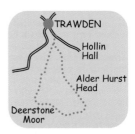

Trawden is a sizeable village with the Trawden Arms and Sun Inn, café and Post office. From St Mary's church take the cul-de-sac road south-east to a phone box and bus turning area. Here go right to a path passing right of the former Literary Institute of 1880. It bears left to emerge at some garages: from the far left corner a snicket rises into a field, continuing enclosed up to a path crossroads at the end of adjacent housing. You shall return down here, but for now turn left across the field to a wall-stile, and with Boulsworth Hill ahead a string of stiles points you towards the house at Slack Laithe. A stile keeps you outside, and above it slant to a wall-stile above. Go left to join a sunken green way between old walls, and follow it right to a cottage. Small gates take you across the front and on to the rear of Naze End. Keep on a wallside path to a gate at the end where you join a cart track. Go left down this to Oaken Bank, and from the houses ahead turn right up a short-lived enclosed path by a stream. This opens out to run on the rear of Alder Hurst Head and on to a gate/stile beyond. In reedy pasture a thin trod follows the left-hand wall away, moistly at times to a stile at the end. Keep straight on, dropping

gently between fences to a gate/stile. Now bear right to Antley Gate (a pile of stones), and a track leads on to quickly rise to a gate/stile onto a firm track on the base of moorland beneath Boulsworth Hill.

Turn right, rising by the wallside. A little higher the wall leaves to return on the brow, above the top end of a plantation. At 1125ft/343m this is the walk's summit alongside a Trawden Forest boundary stone. Here leave the firm track and turn right on a soft one across Deerstone Moor, keeping generally close to the wall. A moist brow brings Pendle Hill and distant Dales heights into view. Forging on, swing left with the wall to arrive above Deerstones just yards to the right: their pleasant top is a good spot for a break. Resume on the track dropping gently towards a corner. Before it, however, take a gate on the right from where a short-lived old way heads off through dry reeds. As it ends at old gateposts in the field, turn right to rise gently with a reedy boundary as far as an old wall. Now drop left on its near side, at the bottom bearing left to a fence-stile. A little path crosses to another then on to a stile into a corner of a wood. After initial moistness a good path heads away through the trees past a curious sculpture.

The path crosses to the right edge for a splendid wall-side stride to a corner where a branch goes left before a house. Advance a few yards further on your path in denser trees then take a wall-stile on the right. A faint grass track crosses to the house at Moss Barn. Pass along the front then follow the drive away, out past a pond to a T-junction with a rough access road. Go briefly right to a stile on the left, and head away with the wall. Passing a mast Trawden returns to the scene, and dropping down when the wall turns off, slant left to rejoin a descending a wall at a stile in it. Don't use it but resume with the wall down two final pastures to rejoin your outward route.

Galloway cattle on Deerstone Moor

Left: Woodland sculpture under Deerstones

4¹⁄4 miles from Trawden

Pick a clear day for this straightforward ascent of a supreme viewpoint

Start Hollin Hall (GR: 916380), roadside parking on cul de-sac half-mile south-east of church

Map OS Explorer OL21, South Pennines

Access Long-established moorland concession path

TRAWDEN

Hollin
Hall

Lumb
Spout

Pot
Brinks
Moor

Gilford
Clough

Boulsworth Hill

New housing occupies the former mill at Hollin Hall. Leave the village by continuing along the road which immediately narrows into a country lane, climbing away then easing out, with Boulsworth looking daunting ahead. At a sharp bend left go straight ahead on a drive to Lodge Moss Farm: keep left of the buildings to a bridle-gate at the end of the yard. A track runs on to another gate, then descends to cross a tree-lined stream. A brief detour down the far bank finds a superb vantage point for the shady hollow enclosing the waterfall of Lumb Spout. Resuming, bear left up a distinct green way, fading as it eases out to cross to a gate/stile at a wall corner. Continue up the wallside behind to rise gently to a stile onto an access road on the base of Pot Brinks Moor. Turn briefly right towards the barns at Spoutley Lumb, then go left up a concrete waterworks road to begin the ascent proper of Boulsworth Hill.

The climb to the summit is an invigorating one. The easy surface is soon relinquished as the path forges uphill, marker posts confirming the route. Beyond an early kissing-gate the path enjoys a steep section, which on easing reveals the summit further to the right. Gentler slopes lead up to Little Chair Stones, and the some-times moist path swings right to slant up to the skyline Weather Stones. This is the best cluster on the walk, featuring some massive boulders. From here rolling moors stretch eastwards across the Pennine watershed to Crow Hill and Withins Height above the head of Walshaw Dean. A two-minute walk south-west across the broad top leads to the waiting Ordnance Survey column. Boulsworth Hill rises as an upturned boat from the rolling moorland, and its lengthy top bristles with an assortment of gritstone outcrops. The summit, Lad Law, is itself a cluster of boulders, and at 1696ft/517m this is one of the principal summits of the South Pennines. Boulsworth's greatest asset as a viewpoint is its 360-degree panorama, which includes the Yorkshire Dales, the Lake District and Bowland.

Return on a path heading west (a little left of Pendle Hill), initially moist but soon reaching scattered boulders around the upright Abbot Stone. From this fine location the ground steepens, and the path transforms into a grassy, peat-free way. Beyond the first of two fence-stiles the last stage accompanies a wall down to rejoin the rough road by way of some moist moments. Go left, but quickly leave by a wall-stile alongside a gate. Head down a vague path on the left side of a broad tongue, overlooking tree-lined Gilford Clough. Well before reaching a confluence, a path slants left down to a footbridge on the stream, and up the other side to a stile beneath a house at Gilford Clough Farm. The path diverts right outside the buildings to emerge onto the driveway beyond. Simply advance along this which in due course leads back to Hollin Hall, absorbing other drives and passing various houses before dropping onto the road.

On Boulsworth Hill

39

3¹4 miles from Nelson

A colourful side valley and an intriguing hamlet

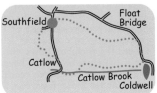

*Start Southfield
(GR: 881371), 1¹2 miles east
of centre above Marsden Park, parking by Shooters Arms
Map OS Explorer OL21, South Pennines*

Sat above the hamlet of Southfield the Shooters Arms boasts a magnificent panorama over the district to the landmark of Pendle Hill. Alongside the pub is a wall-stile into a field: ascending, continue up when the wall turns off. Slant to a stile in the top right corner, with the dome of Boulsworth Hill ahead. Maintain the slant down to another corner stile, erring left to avoid a moist corner. Go right to another corner stile, then contour across unkempt pasture to merge with a fence, passing through a gate near the end and on to a wall-stile. Cross grassy Crawshaw Lane to another stile, then cross the field to one in front of the farm at Ring Stone Hill. Go left of the buildings, over the drive to a stile behind a barn. Now bear left beneath the fence, slanting down to a wall-stile in Pathole Beck's little clough. Across a plank bridge advance to another stile, then slant gently up from the reedy floor to where wall and fence meet ahead. Through a gate/stile advance along the wallside to the farm at Float Bridge. Entering the yard, go left a few yards then take a few steps on the right before the house. A stile takes you out of this tiny garden from where cross a field to a stile onto a road.

Go right, soon rising to a brow and a bend. Just a little further is Coldwell activity centre: formerly the Coldwell Inn, it was notorious for gambling and cockfighting. It closed in 1939 and is now a residential centre with tearoom, WCs and information. The adjacent reservoirs were built in 1884 (lower) and 1935 (upper). At this bend take a kissing-gate to the right to descend a rough corner above water treatment works. Through a kissing-gate at the bottom corner turn right to a gate into the upper valley of Catlow Brook.

The path runs grandly on this spacious clough above the stream, and beyond a fence-stile enters a big rolling section. Approaching a clump of beech trees at an old quarry the path turns right up the steep bank, above the trees to a stile behind. Head away on a splendid course along the rim of a well-defined plunge to the clough floor. Good views look back to Boulsworth Hill, while Pendle Hill returns ahead. Easy going leads on and slowly down to merge with a track on the edge of this vast pasture, and at the end this slants down to a confluence. Cross a footbridge by the stone bridge and follow the track downstream onto the narrow road through Catlow Bottoms.

Cross the stream on a setted ford/stepping-stones before a steep, sunken pull to the hamlet of Catlow. At a crossroads with walled tracks take the inviting one bearing left, with an old quarry to the right. As it swings left take a wall-stile on your right, and follow a wall to a corner stile under the quarry edge. A short walled way runs on beneath the bank, emerging to advance a few yards to a bridle-gate on the left. Escape and descend the wallside to another, then right on a wallside to another corner. From a stile on the right advance a short way to a few steps up to a small gate, and an enclosed path runs on to emerge onto an access road at Southfield House. This is a lovely corner, with three-storey weavers' cottages. John Wesley preached here in 1786, and eleven years later farmer William Sagar converted half of his barn into a Methodist chapel: it still functions, just yards to your left. Turn right on the road up past an enormous quarry hole in woodland back to the waiting pub.

Southfield Methodist Chapel

4¹2 miles from Fence

Undemanding rambling in the historic Forest of Pendle, on a ridge looking to Pendle Hill

Start Fence Gate (GR: 824370), parking by church at west end

Map OS Explorer OL21, South Pennines

Spen Height...

Forest of Pendle

Wheatley Lane

FENCE

Fence is a straggling village that merges with Wheatley Lane in the parish of Old Laund Booth. Just past St Anne's church is the Bay Horse: opposite it a stile sends an enclosed path along to a field. Continue on the hedgeside, rising to a stile behind a tiny stream in the top corner. Rise up another fieldside to a stile onto a road. Go right to Higher Fencegate, and from a gate/stile on the left ascend a field to a small gate and footbridge at the top. Bear right through an intervening stile to a gate near the corner, revealing Pendle Hill and surrounding moors. Turn right on a track towards Rigg of England, but a corner gate/stile see it resume through a broad pasture left of the farm. This fades but cross over the drive and bear right to a corner stile onto a road as it crosses the ridge.

From a gate opposite a drive heads away, merging with another to run past a mast to Higher Spen Farm. Advance on until level with the last building, then take a stile on the left. Bear right through a gate/stile and rejoin the old line to a stile ahead. Head straight past the old farm at Spen Height and on to a fence corner stile. Resume on the other side through two wall-stiles, and maintain a direct line descending slightly through old vaccary walls. Reaching twin stiles at a line of trees the path forks: bear right to keep to the ridge-line, passing a wall corner and on to a gate in a corner behind. Cross a reedy pasture side to a farm drive, turning right over a cattle-grid and out onto a road at Noggarth End. Go briefly left (just further is Noggarth Top Shop, with refreshments) then take a gate on the right to descend the fieldside to a stile in the bottom corner. A short path drops down through another, over a tiny stream and out into a poorly drained field. Slant right down to a stile into the car park of the attractive Sparrowhawk pub.

Go right on the road to the Inghamite Chapel of 1750, then right behind it and onto a path through the graveyard. At the end it becomes enclosed to run to a stile onto an old way. Advance past old farm buildings, beyond which the path emerges onto a drive. Cross to a short enclosed path opposite where a stile puts you into a field at the end. Go right, the enclosed path crossing the field top to emerge onto a drive. Though the main street is just above, instead take an adjacent gate/stile and down a short drive bridging an iron-rich stream. Through a gate keep right of the buildings and an enclosed path resumes past gardens, emerging into a field to continue with a hedge to a stile at the end onto the A6068. Cross to a footway and go a few yards right to a stile in the hedge.

Angle away from the road by an old fence, and over an intervening stile comes a short drop into a wooded gill. Two foot-bridges cross above a confluence, then ascend the bank and bear left outside trees to a stile onto an access road at sports fields. Go right to the clubhouse, then left on an enclosed track past the cricket pitch. Just before the corner take a stile on the right and cross to a kissing-gate in a wall. An enclosed path heads away to emerge onto a road. From a stile opposite resume this line, enclosed until emerging into a field. Keep on to a stile at the far end, then bear right to a kissing-gate in a hedge. This puts you back onto the A6068. Go briefly left towards a junction but cross to a gap that neatly concludes by houses opposite the Fence Gate Inn.

The Sparrowhawk in 1990s livery

4 miles from Higham

**A foray over the ridge dividing
urban Pendle from rural
Pendle, into a hidden valley
where fine old houses nestle**

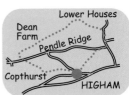

*Start Village centre (GR: 809365), roadside parking
Map OS Explorer OL21, South Pennines*

Leave the village street on a rough lane past the church
hall by St John the Evangelist's church. This becomes a grass track
emerging into a field. A path rises through gorse, then veer right
across this domed pasture to a kissing-gate: ahead is Spence Moor
and part of Pendle Hill. Keep straight on through moist reeds to the
next, then alongside a wide ditch all the way to a gate/stile onto a
back road on Pendle Ridge. Go right to a T-junction then left to the
brow: the hidden valley is at your feet. Ignore a branch right and
drop as far as a drive on the left, and follow this down to Lower
Houses Farm, a beautiful old house with a 1592 datestone.

Advance to a gate in front, and an enclosed green way
heads off, emerging into a colourful pasture with Old House ahead.
The track runs to a ford/slab bridge on a stream, over which cross
a footbridge on an adjacent stream and double back down to a stile.
Head away from it, rounding a gentle brow to a stile in the fence
opposite. Bear right to a wall-stile at the end of the field: over to
the right are Spence Moor's colourful slopes. Head away with the
fence, and when it turns off go straight ahead towards the derelict
farm at Drivers. Pass to the right and down a grassy way towards
the bottom corner. Don't use the gate but turn right on a green
track along the bottom of the field. Below is Sabden Brook, which
performs an ox-bow before it heads away. Ignoring a stile on the
right, keep on to a gate/stile ahead. A track forms to cross to the
far corner of the field then on a fieldside to Dean Farm. A kissing-
gate admits onto the drive. Follow it to the left to reveal a superb
old frontage sporting mullioned windows and a carved inscription.

Resume on the drive heading away, but soon turn off at a footbridge. Crossing Sabden Brook, bear right up the field to the start of a wall. Pass to its right, and as it turns away keep straight on to slant to a stile in the wall ahead, on the slopes of The Height. Turn right on a thin path rising slightly away to a wall-stile. Advance across this pasture to a wall corner ahead, and continue with the wall. At its apex is a junction of green ways: double back left up a distinct rake that fades at the top. Bear right to follow the wall up to a stile back onto the ridge road. Outspread ahead are the South and West Pennine moors. Go left fifty yards to a stile on the right, and slant away from the road across extensive pasture: ahead is Higham. Pass through a couple of old boundary ditches and slant down to a wall opposite, following it right. Before the bottom take a gate in it and join a fence on the right to drop down to Copthurst, a fine old house.

Over a corner wall-stile drop to a stile onto the drive, then cross over it to another. Head away beneath the wall outside its grounds, slanting across to a gate/stile. Cross to a wall-stile ahead, then cross a larger field past a solitary tree to a gate/stile. A faint way heads away to drop to a plank bridge, soon bearing right to a footbridge above a wooded clough in front of housing. A snicket leads onto a suburban street: go left then left again into a cul-de-sac, taking an enclosed path right to emerge into playing fields. Cross to an access track at the other side out onto a road, going right to re-enter the main street at the Four Alls pub and the old village water supply.

Sabden Brook

4¹⁄4 miles from Sabden

A bracing tramp over moorland on the southern flanks of Pendle Hill

Start Village centre
(GR: 779374), car park
Map OS Explorer 287, West Pennine Moors

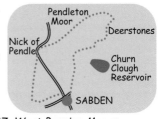

Sabden is a pleasant village with the Pendle Witch and White Hart pubs, café, Post office, shop and antiques centre. From the central crossroads turn right on Wesley Street for St Nicholas' church: dating from 1846, its thin tower tapers to a spire. Before reaching it turn left on a lane for Badger Wells Cottages. This rises to a junction at Cockshotts Farm. Go left over the stream and up to the front of the terrace. To the right an enclosed path rises to a gate at the top. The next stages of the walk appear high above as Deerstones break the skyline beyond attractive Churn Clough. An inviting path heads straight up the pasture, through a kissing-gate at the top corner and resuming alongside a small stream. Grand strides lead up to a kissing-gate onto the foot of grassy moor.

The path rises a little further to meet a cart track. Turn right on this, using gates to pass briefly through a field-top to rejoin the moor. With Churn Clough Reservoir below, it runs on to cross a tree-lined stream. Winding round the bank opposite it runs on again, now as a path, through a gate towards a plantation. Crossing another sidestream beneath new plantings, ignore a stile into the wood and follow the path uphill, leaving the trees behind. Climbing through bracken with Deerstones ahead, keep left at a fork, crossing a tiny stream with the steep-sided clough on the left. The path shrugs off bracken and scales the broad shoulder falling from Deerstones. As the edge is gained, a fine prospect opens out westwards to Longridge Fell and the southern Bowland moors. While the now thinner main path goes directly ahead towards a wall, make use of a still thinner right branch scaling the modest edge to quickly reach its highest point. The few minor out-crops at Deerstones overlook a deep, boulder-filled amphitheatre.

Resume by dropping briefly back down the path to quickly bear right on a level path contouring to a gate in the wall just ahead. A good path heads away, initially level then dropping and curving left: ignore a cross-path just prior to merging into the wide Pendle ascent path on its broad ridge. Go left for a grand stride down this prolonged, gentle decline all the way to the crest of the Sabden-Clitheroe road at its 985ft/300m summit on the Nick of Pendle. During this spell Clitheroe is seen down to the right beneath Waddington Fell, backed by stretches of the Bowland moors.

Go left down the verge just as far as a gate on the right, and follow a drive away as far as Parsley Barn. After it bear left down rough pasture to a gate/stile at the bottom, then drop to the start of a wall: across the tiny stream a good wallside path forms between it and the broadening wooded gill. Through a gate/stile at the bottom the broader way slants right, down to the far end of a group of buildings. From a gate on the left pass along the front of the first and then on an enclosed green way to a driveway between houses at The Whins. Go briefly right, then take a wall-stile on the left. A grassy way heads off along the field bottom, rising slightly at the end to a kissing-gate. A thinner way resumes, again rising slightly to run on to a gate onto the road at the village edge. Go right down the footway back into the centre.

Deerstones

HILLSIDE GUIDES... cover much of Northern England

Other colour *Pocket Walks* guides (more in preparation)

·UPPER WHARFEDALE ·LOWER WHARFEDALE
·UPPER WENSLEYDALE ·LOWER WENSLEYDALE
·MALHAMDALE ·SWALEDALE ·RIBBLESDALE
·INGLETON/WESTERN DALES ·SEDBERGH/DENTDALE
·NIDDERDALE ·HARROGATE/KNARESBOROUGH
·BOWLAND ·AROUND PENDLE ·RIBBLE VALLEY
·AMBLESIDE/LANGDALE ·BORROWDALE
·AIRE VALLEY ·ILKLEY/WASHBURN VALLEY

Our *Walking Country* range features more great walks...

·WHARFEDALE ·MALHAMDALE ·WENSLEYDALE
·HARROGATE & the WHARFE VALLEY ·SWALEDALE
·RIPON & LOWER WENSLEYDALE ·NIDDERDALE
·THREE PEAKS ·HOWGILL FELLS ·HOWARDIAN HILLS
·TEESDALE ·EDEN VALLEY ·ALSTON & ALLENDALE

·ILKLEY MOOR ·BRONTE COUNTRY ·CALDERDALE
·PENDLE & the RIBBLE ·WEST PENNINE MOORS
·ARNSIDE & SILVERDALE ·LUNESDALE ·BOWLAND

·LAKELAND FELLS, SOUTH ·LAKELAND FELLS, EAST
·LAKELAND FELLS, NORTH ·LAKELAND FELLS, WEST

Long Distance Walks

·COAST TO COAST WALK ·CUMBRIA WAY ·DALES WAY
·LADY ANNE'S WAY ·NIDDERDALE WAY
·WESTMORLAND WAY ·FURNESS WAY
·PENDLE WAY ·BRONTE WAY ·CALDERDALE WAY

Visit www.hillsidepublications.co.uk
or write for a catalogue